FIESTA!

F I L

W
FRANKLIN WATTS
NEW YORK • LONDON • SYDNEY

First published 1998
This edition first published 2001

Franklin Watts
96 Leonard Street
London EC2A 4XD

0 7496 4030 8

Dewey Decimal Classification Number: 394.2

A CIP catalogue record for this book is available from the British Library

Copyright © 1997 Times Media Pte Ltd, Singapore

Originated by Marshall Cavendish Books
an imprint of Times Media Pte Ltd
Times Centre, 1 New Industrial Road, Singapore 536196

Second Printing 2001

Brown Partworks Limited
Editorial Staff
Series Editor: Tessa Paul
Series Designer: Joyce Mason
Crafts devised and created by Susan Moxley
Music arrangements by Harry Boteler
Photographs by Bruce Mackie
Subeditor: Roz Fischel
Production: Alex Mackenzie
Stylists: Joyce Mason and Tessa Paul

For this volume:
Writer: Lesley Dore
Consultant: High Commission for Pakistan, London
Editorial Assistants: Hannah Beardon and Paul Thompson

Printed in Italy

Adult supervision advised for all crafts and recipes
particularly those involving sharp instruments and heat.

CONTENTS

PAKISTAN:

Pakistan is a wedge of land bordered by four countries. To the west are Iran and Afghanistan; to the north and east are China and India. To the south, Pakistan's coastline is on the Arabian Sea.

First Impressions

- **Population** 130,129,000
- **Largest city** Karachi, with a population of 7,702,000
- **Longest river** Indus
- **Highest mountain** Tirig Mir at 7,690 metres
- **Exports** Cotton, carpets, rice, clothing
- **Capital city** Islamabad
- **Political status** Republic
- **Climate** Dry, hot months with seasonal monsoon rains
- **Art and culture** Fine, tiled architecture; wooden carvings, brasswork, exquisite handwoven carpets.

Oman

◀ **This country was born** in 1947 as a 'homeland' for the Muslim peoples of British India. Millions were moved from their homes in India to the new country. Thousands died in the civil unrest that followed the moves. This history has made the people proud and devout Muslims.

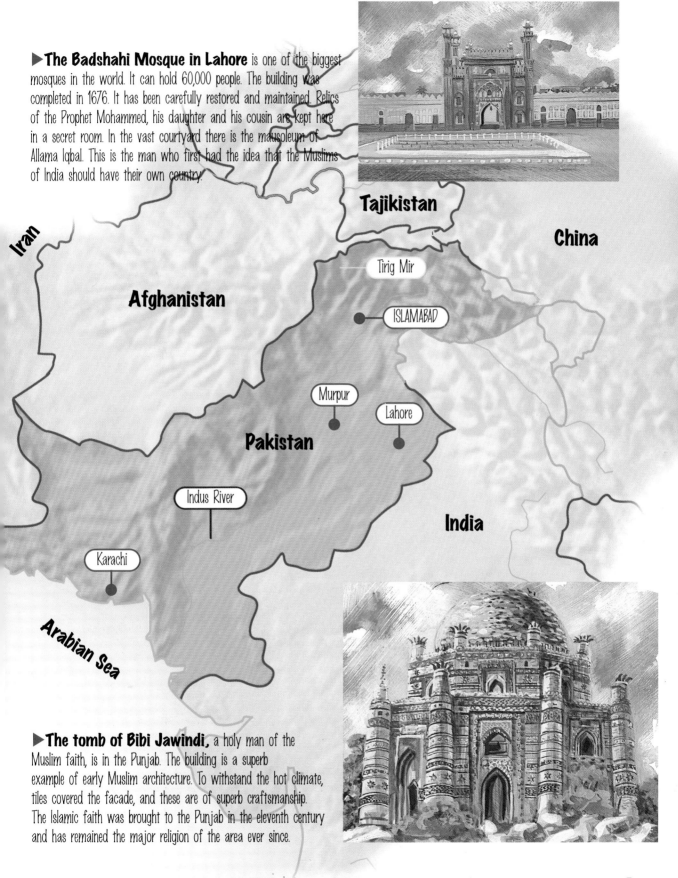

▶ **The Badshahi Mosque in Lahore** is one of the biggest mosques in the world. It can hold 60,000 people. The building was completed in 1676. It has been carefully restored and maintained. Relics of the Prophet Mohammed, his daughter and his cousin are kept here in a secret room. In the vast courtyard there is the mausoleum of Allama Iqbal. This is the man who first had the idea that the Muslims of India should have their own country.

Iran

Tajikistan

China

Afghanistan

Tirig Mir

● ISLAMABAD

Murpur ●

Lahore ●

Pakistan

Indus River

India

Karachi ●

Arabian Sea

▶ **The tomb of Bibi Jawindi,** a holy man of the Muslim faith, is in the Punjab. The building is a superb example of early Muslim architecture. To withstand the hot climate, tiles covered the facade, and these are of superb craftsmanship. The Islamic faith was brought to the Punjab in the eleventh century and has remained the major religion of the area ever since.

RELIGIONS

The British Empire, which had ruled India for centuries, gave that country its independence in 1947. However, Indian Muslims wanted to form their own nation, so Pakistan was created as a Muslim state.

ALMOST ALL PAKISTANIS belong to the Islamic faith founded by the Prophet Mohammed. He was born in the Arabian city of Mecca in AD 570. He thought there was only one god, Allah, and everyone should believe in Him.

Mohammed was visited by an angel who told him he was to be the messenger of Allah. After this Mohammed spent his time teaching, and he found many followers. These Muslims fought against those who worshipped idols and who did not lead a pure life. By the time Mohammed died in 632 in the city of Medina, the religion of Islam was established.

In the years following Mohammed's death, there were quarrels among the Muslims. Some thought Mohammed's

son-in-law should be their leader. This group, the Shi'ah Muslims, split away from the Sunni Muslims.

The majority of Pakistanis are Sunnis. There are a small number of Shi'ahs and also some Ismailis. This sect is an offshoot of the Shi'ahs who follow the hereditary leader, the Aga Khan. Islam first reached the coast of Pakistan in 709 and spread slowly. By the sixteenth century this faith had reached the Western mountains.

Islam is the state religion. Many of the festivals recall events in the history of Islam. They fall on different dates each year. The Muslim calendar is based on changes in the moon, not the sun, so the year is about 11 days shorter than a Western year.

GREETINGS FROM **PAKISTAN!**

Pakistan was part of India and the British Empire until 1947. In that year India became independent, and those areas of the country with a Muslim majority were made into a separate state. The problem was that this new state was in two parts, West and East, divided by thousands of miles of Indian territory. It was difficult for one government to rule them. Eventually the two parts of Pakistan fought a war and in 1972 East Pakistan broke away to become the state of Bangladesh.

Urdu is the official language and is taught in schools, even though few Pakistanis use it as their mother tongue. They speak over two dozen languages, depending on where they come from. Punjabi is the most widely spoken, and educated people in the towns also know English.

How do you say...

Hello

Salaam alay kum

How are you?

Aapka kya hal heyh?

My name is

Mera naam ... hai

Goodbye

Khooda haafiz

Thank you

Shukria

Peace

Salaam

HAJJ AND ID-UL-ADHA

Every Muslim yearns to make the pilgrimage to Mecca. Every year thousands of people meet in Mecca to remember Mohammed.

Each year more than 60,000 people from Pakistan make a special pilgrimage to Mecca, in Arabia, where Mohammed was born. This particular journey is called the *Hajj*. It is made by Muslims from all over the world in *Dhul-Hijjah*, the last month of the Muslim year. Every Muslim longs to visit Mecca at least once in their life.

The people of Pakistan are mostly farmers who grow only enough food to feed their families. A trip to Mecca is difficult because it is hard to find money, or the time to leave their crops. Often families pool all their money just to send one member of the family to Mecca. Sometimes the state helps by providing

The Great Mosque in Mecca is the major holy site of the Muslim faith. It is the birthplace of the Prophet Mohammed. Muslims hope that, if they visit Mecca, Allah will forgive them all their sins.

some free tickets for planes and ships. In the olden days the journey was long and difficult because the pilgrims travelled by camel caravan across the desert to Mecca. There was also a long sea route.

Somebody going to Mecca prepares for the holy trip with rituals of cleanliness. They start to wear white clothes without jewellery. The women must cover their heads. They are invited to huge meals around the village, and are given gifts, usually of money. When the time comes for the pilgrims to leave, the quays and air-port at Karachi are filled with families who come to wave their farewells. Sometimes the entire village is there for the occasion.

During the journey pilgrims pass the time reading the Koran and praying to Allah. When they reach the city of Mecca they stay in

Before aeroplanes, hundreds of pilgrims trekked through the desert to reach Mecca. Their camels were loaded with food and clothes for the journey.

THE ROUTE OF THE HAJJ

When the pilgrims arrive at Mecca, they camp at Mina. They prepare by changing into simple white clothes.

On entering Mecca, Muslims walk seven times round the Kaaba, a huge, cube-shaped building said to be built by Ibrahim. They pray at the Great Mosque, where Mohammed was born, and collect holy Zamzam water from the well in its courtyard.

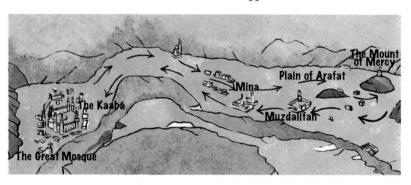

Finally, they cross the Plain of Arafat to hear a sermon about Mohammed on the Mount of Mercy. All Muslims make this special Hajj once in their lives.

Gifts from Mecca are treasured. Dates from Medina, the desert town near the holy site, are said to be the best in the world. Beautiful Korans are always appreciated by the faithful.

tents that have been prepared for them. More than 2,000,000 people visit the holy site every year so there are vast crowds to be seen in every direction.

The first place the pilgrims go to in Mecca is the *Kaaba*. This is a building shaped like a huge cube. It is covered with a giant black cloth that is beautifully embroidered. This cloth is cut up into pieces at the end of each Hajj and the pilgrims buy pieces to take home with them. Inside the Kaaba is a room with writings

The return of the pilgrim from Mecca is a happy event. In the villages of Pakistan, the women prepare special foods and wear their best for the fortunate traveller.

from the Koran worked on the walls.

Pilgrims in their thousands circle the Kaaba seven times. They pray and then they run seven times between two hills near the Kaaba. They do this to remember the fact that the wife of the prophet Ibrahim, or Abraham, ran this way looking for water for her baby.

The *wuquf* is the next part of the Hajj. Wuquf means 'stand before Allah'. Pilgrims stand from midday until sunset, praying to Allah.

Then they celebrate *Id-ul-Adha*, to recall how, long ago, Ibrahim prepared to sacrifice Ismail, his son, to Allah. They say prayers and kill a sheep or goat, giving the life of the animal to Allah.

There are three more days of ritual and then most pilgrims travel home. In the towns and villages of Pakistan the returning pilgrims are greeted with parties. They bring presents from the holy place. Everyone shares the joy of those who have completed the most important of all journeys in a pious Muslim's life.

ZAMZAM WATER

The Well of Zamzam is in the courtyard of the Great Mosque in Mecca. Muslims believe this well was shown to Hajar, the wife of Ibrahim, when she was lost in the desert. Her baby was crying with thirst so she searched for water, but fell, exhausted, between the desert hills. Allah heard her son cry and made a spring bubble up between his fingers. When pilgrims are on the Hajj, they drink as much of the wellwater as they can. Pilgrims dip their white clothes in it. They take the cloth home to be used to wrap their bodies in when they die. They take home bottles of water and cakes of mud from the spring as souvenirs and gifts for their loved ones.

EID-UL-FITR

Muslims prove their faith by fasting during the month of Ramadan. The end of the fast is celebrated with **Eid-ul-Fitr,** *a joyous festival of food and presents.*

For Eid, Muslims wear new clothes. The girls receive jewellery.

Eid-ul-Fitr is the festival that celebrates the end of Ramadan, the month when Muslims do not eat or drink anything between sunrise and sunset. The difficult act of fasting shows that the truly faithful will suffer gladly for Allah.

Children, pregnant women, the elderly and people on a journey do not fast. Ramadan lasts a month and ends with the feast of Eid-ul-Fitr.

This Eid lasts three days. People prepare for it by buying gifts for each other. They give money to the poor to make sure they can enjoy the Eid as well.

The festival begins when the new moon appears, showing that the new month has begun. Some people do not go to bed that night. They stay up with friends and watch for the moon.

NABI NABI

Na-bi Na-bi — Na-bi Na-bi — Na-bi Na-bi — Na-bi Na-bi —

Na-bi Na-bi — Na-bi Na-bi — Na-bi Na-bi — Na-bi Na-bi —

This is a chant from a Pakistani song. The singers and musicians improvise as they play. This means they alter the words and notes as they perform. The music can still be recognised, but it alters a little each time.

Families wake up early on Eid morning. They put on new clothes as Mohammed wore new clothes at Eid. The mosques are crowded. People meet and embrace friends and greet each other with Eid blessings. They visit relatives and friends to feast and exchange Eid gifts.

Greeting cards adorned with beautiful writing are sent to friends and family during this festival.

URS

*The **Sufis**, the holy men of the Muslims, are remembered in huge festivals. These are known as **urs** and they happen each year at the holy man's shrine or tomb.*

All over the country there are sites dedicated to *Sufis*, or Muslim holy men who have spent pious lives in prayer. There are no saints in the Muslim faith. However, in Pakistan the people regard certain Sufis with much the same awe that Christians give to their saints.

There is a shrine near Karachi to the thirteenth-century Sufi Mangho Pir, but one of the most famous is at Schwan Shary. Here a tomb covered in blue tiles has become the shrine of a scholar-poet, Lal Shahba Qalandar, who came from Persia in the twelfth century.

Each year a huge urs, or religious festival, marks the anniversary of the poet's death. It lasts for three days, and thousands of people attend the event.

Many pilgrims bring offerings to Sufi shrines. They bring scarves, cloths or incense. Men selling water mingle in the crowd gathered for the urs, and food stalls are set up everywhere.

SUFIS

Sufi comes from the Arabic word meaning 'purity'. Sufis started in Persia in the ninth century. Many were poets, scholars and musicians. They lived simply — fasting, praying and converting people to Islam. They preached a message of love, peace and brotherhood. They obeyed no one but Allah, refusing to obey even monarchs. The places where Sufis settled and died are places of pilgrimage. Shrines are built at their tombs and people bring offerings of flowers, fruit and money.

The noise at the festival is deafening. Drums and gongs beat as thousands of pilgrims dance and sing. The crowd is thrilled by the dancing dervishes. They are Sufis who show their faith through dance.

In Nurpur, close to Islamabad city, is the shrine of the Sufi Syed Abdul Latif Shah. The shrine is under a huge, shady banyan tree.

At Syed Abdul Latif Shah's urs each spring there is a fairground with side shows. People sing and dance for days in memory of this holy man. Many pilgrims come to his shrine for miracles. They hang locks of hair on the banyan tree or smear ash on their foreheads and wounds. They hope their lame limbs or their illnesses will be cured in this way.

The Sufi Mangho Pir has a shrine near a pool of crocodiles. Pilgrims think the crocodiles are holy, so the animals are treated with care and are fed by the visitors. Dancing dervishes belong to a branch of Sufism. They wear wide skirts and conical hats (above).

15

THE STORY OF MANGHO PIR

A pious Muslim visited Mecca but he felt a strong urge to travel across the desert. He believed Allah wanted him to trek to foreign shores. Allah did lead him to a new land, where the man's goodness inspired miracles and love.

LONG AGO A HOLY man named Mangho Pir walked through the deserts of Arabia. While he stumbled across the hot sands, he thought longingly of the holy city of Mecca and the waters of Zamzam. He prayed that before night came Allah would lead him to an oasis.

Mangho Pir knew he must keep travelling. He fasted and prayed. He met some nomads with their camels and tents. 'Travel with us,' the nomads said. Mangho Pir replied, 'I must cross the mountains you see in the East. Then I must cross water that stretches away like the sand.'

When he reached the mountains, he found that it was very cold there. He was glad his hair had grown long and thick, for it kept him warm at night. At last he came to the sea and some fishermen took him in their boat to Pakistan. He landed on the islands where Karachi now stands.

All day he walked and at night he lay down to sleep. He dreamed this was the place where he must stay. When he awoke he was in despair because he was in a dry, terrible place. He picked up a stick and beat the ground, crying, 'Oh, Allah, why must this place be my home?'

Out of the sand sprang two oases with shady trees and grass. From a clump of date palms gushed hot springs giving off the smell of sulphur. As Mangho Pir shook his head in amazement, the lice living in his long hair fell out and jumped into the water. They turned into crocodiles. When he bent to wash in the warm water, his tired hands were soothed and healed.

The fame of this good man and his crocodiles guarding the sulphurous waters spread far. Today thousands of pilgrims still come to Mangho Pir's shrine to seek cures for their skin diseases and to offer goats to the holy crocodiles that continue to live there.

MAKE A MOSAIC

Here is a bird design typical of Pakistan, but you can make any image you like. Keep it simple. Remember, the design must be made of straight lines to carry the little square or oblong mosaics.

In Pakistan there are many buildings with beautiful tile and mosaic work. Sufi shrines are often carefully maintained, and either tiles or mosaics are used to ornament Sufi tombs and the shrines. Mosaics are a very old craft. The Ancient Romans were particularly fond of mosaics. They used chips of glass and coloured stone. Some craftsmen are very skilled and use curved, round and irregular shapes to build a mosaic picture.

YOU WILL NEED
Air-hardening clay
Aluminium foil
Blunt knife
All-purpose glue
Paintbrush
Poster paints
Cardboard about 20 cm x 20 cm
Ruler
Coloured pencils
Picture ring

1 Roll out clay on aluminium foil in an oblong 20 cm x 20 cm. Mark into 2cm squares, almost cutting through the clay. Allow clay to dry. Varnish with all-purpose glue.

2 Paint the clay with the poster paints. Block areas of squares and paint the colours required. Allow to dry.

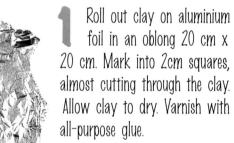

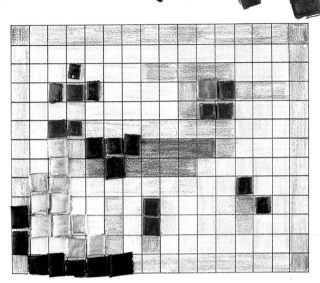

3 Take cardboard and draw lines about 2 cm apart horizontally and vertically. Colour in the design with coloured pencils. Paint all-purpose glue on small section of cardboard.

4 Break off squares of clay and press each onto a square of the glued cardboard, matching mosaic to colour design. Glue a ring to the back of the mosaic and hang it up as a picture or use it to decorate a table.

PUL HARVEST

The Kalasha are not Muslim, Christian or Hindu. They worship spirits and deities. These people work hard to grow food and thank the gods of the crops with great harvest festivals.

In the valleys of Chitral, lonely and isolated by the border of Afghanistan, live the Kalasha people. They love music and dancing, especially during the seasonal festivals held to celebrate the harvest of their crops.

They eat little meat, and their lives depend on growing enough food for the months ahead. They rejoice when the grains are safely stored in summer or when the fruits are ripe in autumn. They make sacrifices and give praise to their gods.

The Kalasha decorate their shrines, homes and coffins with elaborate woodcarving. They always dress in black but beads, buttons and coins add some colour. Festive costumes are decorated with buttons and colourful stitching.

These people believe in a great creator, Dezau. They also worship the god Mahandeo, who protects crops and animals, and the goddess Jestak, who cares for the family. There are shrines to these gods all over the valleys. The dead are not buried but rest on the ground in graveyards.

The Kalasha use dance to express what is important to them. There are dances to mark and celebrate births, marriages and deaths. In a typical dance the older men stand in the centre chanting old legends.

As the drums beat, the women dance around them, arms around one another's waists.

In September or early October these people dance nonstop to mark Pul, the walnut and grape harvest, and the end of winemaking. Many visitors trek to this remote area for the festival.

The Kalasha grow wheat and barley. They do not have modern machinery and work hard to cut and thresh the grain themselves. Their gnarled grapevines grow on trees, and the picking of the fruit is celebrated in autumn.

21

MILAD-UL-NABI

Milad-ul-Nabi *is the Prophet Mohammed's birthday. The day is devoted to children. They are told stories and have fun.*

In July or August there is a public holiday to celebrate the the prophet's birthday. Offices and all schools close. People like to be with their families as this festival, *Milad-ul-Nabi*, is regarded as a day for children.

Children put on their best clothes. They may go to the *madrash*, a special school run by the mosque. All the small children gather together and sit on the ground, but after the age of 12, the boys and girls sit apart. The men and women never sit together in the mosques.

The madrash teaches the children to read and write in Arabic, so that they can study the Koran, the holy book of the Muslims. It is written in Arabic, which is the language that was spoken by Mohammed.

Pious Muslim homes display sayings from the Koran. These may be embroidered or painted. The Arabic calligraphy, or writing, makes beautiful designs. Boys wear decorative caps. Girls cover their heads with pretty scarves.

The wisdom of the Koran comes directly from Allah, and the words of the prophet are recorded in a book called *Hadith*. Muslims turn to both these holy books for moral lessons.

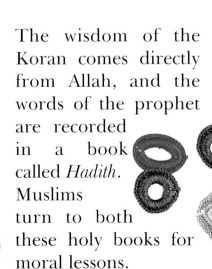

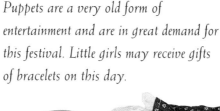

Puppets are a very old form of entertainment and are in great demand for this festival. Little girls may receive gifts of bracelets on this day.

During Milad-ul-Nabi all children are told stories about Mohammed, his childhood as a shepherd boy in the desert and how the angel Gabriel brought him messages from God. They learn about other great Islamic leaders, such as the prophets Moses and Ibrahim.

After mosque or madrash the children go home to a special meal with their family. In the villages there are entertainments, sweets and games to please the little ones. There are not many cinemas or theatres in rural Pakistan, but puppet shows and circuses travel around from village to village.

SWEET LASSI

SERVES TWO

10 oz. (285 g) natural yoghurt
Glass of water
Honey
Pinch of cinnamon
Ice cubes

Put the yoghurt and water in a jug. Add honey to taste and a pinch of cinnamon. Add the ice cubes. Use a hand mixer to blend the ingredients together and crush the ice cubes. Serve immediately.

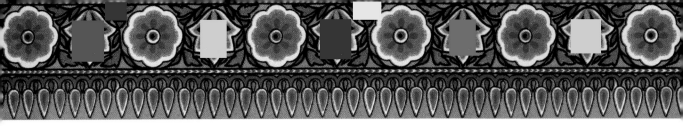

MOSES AND THE WISE MAN

This story comes from the Koran. It is a moral tale often read to

Muslim children. It explains why there is suffering in the world,

and that the will of Allah is always wise.

ONE DAY THE PROPHET Moses came upon a wise man who was a true servant of Allah because Allah had given him the gift of knowledge. 'Can I follow you and learn what you know?' asked Moses. But the Wise Man was not sure. 'I don't think you will have the patience.' But Moses promised to be patient and obedient and the Wise Man agreed to let him travel with him, as long as Moses did not ask any questions.

They set out on their journey. Soon they came to a ship. The wise man bored a hole in the bottom of the ship. 'What have you done?' asked

Moses. 'Do you want to drown all the passengers?'

'I told you not to ask questions.'

Moses apologised and fell silent. The two travelled on until they met a young man. The wise man killed him. Moses was shocked. 'That was a terrible thing to do!' he cried. 'Why did you kill an innocent man?'

'I told you not ask questions.'

'I'm sorry,' Moses said. 'I will not question you again.'

They reached a town where no one would give them food or shelter. As they left, the wise man stopped and repaired a falling wall. 'Huh!' said

Moses. 'You should have asked them for something in return for that work.'

The wise man turned to Moses. 'I will explain my actions. A king was going to steal the ship but those men need it to make their living. With a hole it is useless to the king, but the men will mend it and go on using it. The death of the young man spared his parents the dreadful suffering he was about to cause. Now they will have another son, who will be good to them. As for the wall, a treasure is buried beneath it. It is Allah's will that two orphans will find the treasure when they grow up, because their father was a good man. I acted according to Allah's will.'

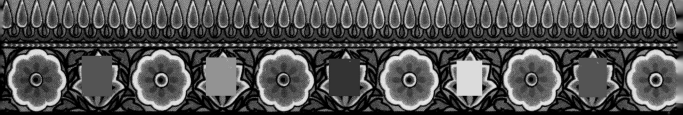

SHAHI DURBAR

A fair has grown around an old meeting place. Traditional pastimes and new ways of farming mix in a grand display.

The town of Sibi in the southwest of Pakistan is one of the hottest places in the whole of the sub-continent. The people are mainly nomadic.

In summer they move with their flocks of animals up to the cool mountains. Before the heat of summer sets in and the nomads' trek to the hills begins, a famous fair is held in Sibi. It is called the *Shahi Durbar*. The fair begins mid-February and it lasts for a week.

'Durbar' means 'royal meeting' and the tradition probably started in the fifteenth century when tribal chiefs would assemble to discuss regional matters. Today it has become an important agricultural fair.

People come from far afield to show their livestock and exhibit their produce, crafts and traditional skills.

Preparations for the fair start as early as January. Thousands of people gather in Sibi. The fair starts

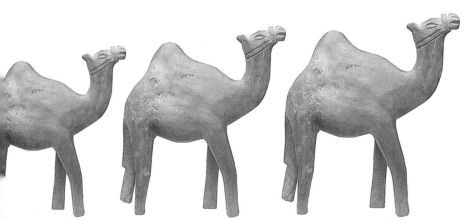

Camels are extremely important to the desert people. At the Durbar the best of these animals are exhibited. Elephants and horses are also important to the farmers. Craftsmen model these animals in wood or embroidered cloth.

OLD SPORT

Polo is an ancient team game played on horseback. It began in northern Pakistan and is played on a grass field with wooden goal posts that break if a horse runs into them. The riders hold mallets to hit the ball. Many festivals are celebrated with polo matches. Spectators shout and cheer. Clarinets and drums add to the din. Coaches send musical messages to players just as, in olden days, kings directed their troops into battle by signalling with different tunes.

with a horse and cattle show in which the best animals win rosettes and are sold for a high price. The nomadic people of Balachistan come with camels and horses. These people are famous for their horse-riding and they give daring displays of their skills at the fair. There are also shows of tribal dancing, polo and wrestling.

Craft stalls sell embroidered silks, clothes, toys covered with mirrors, pretty boxes and pottery. Kebabs are on sale everywhere.

For seven days Sibi is full of activity, colour and noise.

Humpbacked cattle can be seen at the Durbar. The breed is called Brahmin and it is suited to local farming methods. In the hills of the north, men still hunt with falcons, as they have for centuries, and other old sports, such as wrestling, thrill the Durbar crowds.

MAKE A FELT HAT

Delight a friend by giving an unusual present. This decorative hat is easy to make and fun to wear.

The men and boys of Pakistan wear hats like this one. It is traditional to wear such hats when attending mosque. Some are crocheted or quite simple in design. Others, made for festive occasions, are decorated with embroidery and mirrors. The hat sits on the top of the head.

YOU WILL NEED
Scissors
1 m felt
Red, orange, white and green wool
Darning needle
Buttons
Aluminium foil

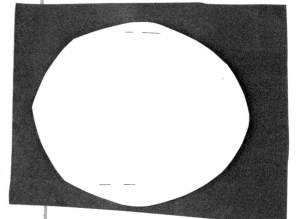

1 For the crown, measure head size. Cut an oval shape to fit. For the rim, measure circumference of crown. Cut a length of felt to fit circumference. Fold length at centre and, cutting through both thicknesses, cut pointed arch shape (see above).

2 Use white wool and darning needle to tack ends of the rim together, and then to tack around bottom edge, following the line of the arch cut-out. Use red wool to tack between the stitches of the white wool.

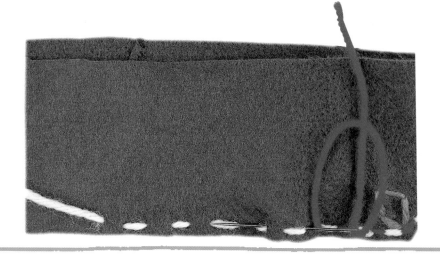

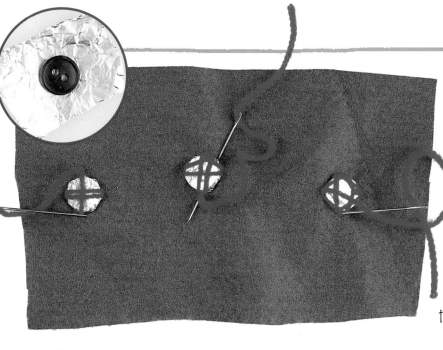

3 Cover the first button in aluminium foil. Position on hat. Stitch by sewing a double cross in red wool over the covered button. To finish, bring needle out at base of one of the crosses, catch thread in the centre and stitch back into the same base. Attach all buttons needed for the design using this method.

4 Stitch on orange thread, using large stitches to create diamond shapes as shown in the diagram.

5 Fit crown to rim and stitch together with green wool using blanket stitch (far right). To make blanket stitch, push needle through rim and through edge of crown. Before pulling the wool taut, thread needle through the stitch, then through fabric of rim and crown. Repeat.

ASHURA

Ashura *is a day of mourning for the death of Hussein, the prophet's grandson. It is specially significant to the Shi'ah Muslims.*

The Muslim world is divided between Sunni Muslims and Shi'ah, or Shi'ite, Muslims. The two groups quarrel over the status and rights of Mohammed's early family.

The Shi'ah Muslims particularly honour Hussein, Mohammed's grandson. Hussein died a terrible death in the desert. He and his men died from the wounds of battle and of thirst. In Pakistan the Shi'ah show their grief for this holy man by acts that make them, the faithful, suffer too. Men and boys form a procession behind a white horse that has no rider. They beat their chests while chanting, over and over again, the names of Hussein and all those who died with him.

WORDS TO KNOW

Fast: To go without some or all kinds of food and drink deliberately.

Dancing dervish: A Muslim who has taken vows of poverty and shows his or her faith through dance.

Incense: A mixture of gum and spice, often shaped into thin sticks or cones, that gives off a pleasant smell when burned.

Koran: The Islamic holy book, believed to be the word of God as told to the prophet Mohammed.

Mecca: The birthplace of Mohammed. Mecca is the most important place of pilgrimage for Muslims.

Mosque: A place of worship for Muslims.

Muslim: A follower of the religion of Islam.

Nomads: People who travel all or some of the time in search of food for their animals.

Oasis: A fertile place within an arid region such as a desert.

Pilgrim: A person who makes a religious journey, or pilgrimage, to a holy place.

Polo: A team game, similar to hockey, played on horseback with long-handled mallets.

Prophet: A teacher or interpreter of the will of God.

Ramadan: The ninth month of the Muslim year, during which Muslims fast from dawn until sunset.

Sacrifice: To give up something that is greatly valued for an even more important reason.

Shi'ahs: A group of Muslims who believe descendants of Mohammed's grandson, Hussein, are his rightful successors.

Shrine: A place that is sacred to the memory of a holy person.

Sufi: A Muslim holy man.

Sunnis: A group of Muslims who believe that the four elected rulers of Islam are Mohammed's rightful successors.

ACKNOWLEDGEMENTS

WITH THANKS TO:
Turkman Gallery, London.
Articles of Faith.
Folk doll by Zoë Paul.

PHOTOGRAPHY:
Photographs by Bruce Mackie and White Backgrounds.
Cover photograph by Getty Images/Keren Su.

ILLUSTRATIONS BY:
Fiona Saunders pp. 4–5. Tracy Rich p. 7. Robert Shadbolt p. 9.
Maps by John Woolford.

Recipe: Roz Fischel.

Index